Imagine ... Amazing Me!

by Libbi Chilia

Editor Diana Donlon
Bryant of Georgia photographed by Brenda Cooper

To contact the author write:
Libbi Chilia
P.O. Box 30566
Middleburg Hts., Ohio 44130

or visit:
www.shoutlife.com/libbichilia
www.halopublishing.com

Halo
Publishing International®
www.halopublishing.com
6415 Granger Road, Independence, Ohio 44131

Dedicated to my Sami who amazes me beyond my imagination.

– Libbi

Anna, age 7, Ohio

"It must be really hard to be a person who has a disability. Glad I don't."

Anna who has both upper and lower limb differences, said this to her mother after playing with other children at a Shriner's facility.

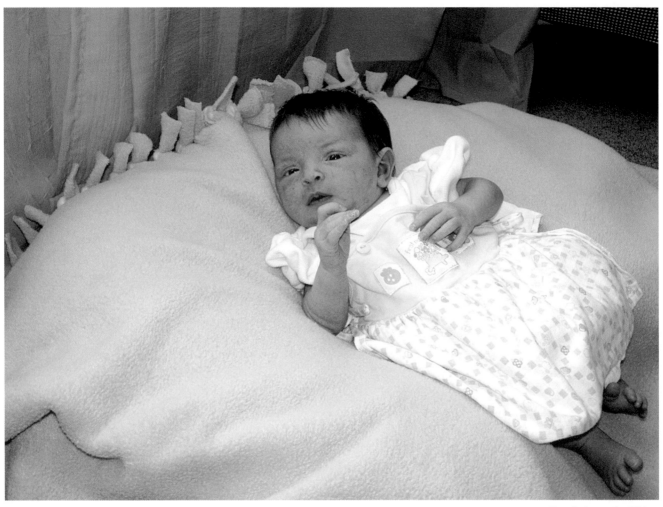

Sami, 1 week, Ohio

When I was born you had so many dreams for me.

You'll be amazed
at all I can do.

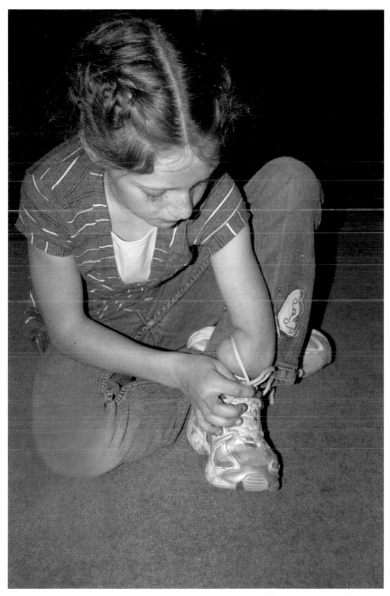

Megan, age 8, Alaska

BJ, age 6, Virginia

I will play you a song,

play basketball,

Megan, age 6, Alaska

Gabriel, age 4, Canada

or soccer...
all day long.

Logan, age 2, Washington

Whatever it is, I will amaze you!

John, age 3, Virginia

I will play in the sand,

or do a handstand,

BJ, age 6, Virginia

or my passion
may be ballet.

Kayla, age 4, Washington

Whatever it is,
I know I will amaze you!

Mercedes, age 7, Missouri

Samir, age 6, Arizona

I'll paint you a picture,

chase the cat,

Olivia, age 1, New Jersey

Bryant, age 1, Georgia

or enjoy a picnic on a beautiful day.

Jerome, age 3, New York

Whatever I do, I will amaze you!

Scotty, age 4, New York

I may love baseball,

Owen, age 1, Alaska

reading books,

Megan, age 8, Alaska

or playing games.

Shelby, age 1, Ohio

Everything I do will amaze you!

Sami, age 1, Ohio

I'll reach the
top of the slide,

Berklee, age 2, Texas

the tree house,

Sean, age 8, Georgia

and the monkey bars!

I wonder,
did you ever
imagine how
amazing
I would be?

Sami, age 1, Ohio

Keoni, age 1, California

For support
or for more
information about
children with limb
differences, please
visit these sites:

www.pffd.org
www.child-amputee.net
www.amcsupport.org
www.paralympic.org
www.extremitygames.com
www.groups.yahoo.com/
   group/AdoptingChildren-
   WithLimbDifferences